First World War
and Army of Occupation
War Diary
France, Belgium and Germany

57 DIVISION
Headquarters, Branches and Services
Commander Royal Artillery
6 September 1915 - 28 February 1916

WO95/2968/1-2

The Naval & Military Press Ltd
www.nmarchive.com
Published in association with The National Archives

Published by

The Naval & Military Press Ltd

Unit 10 Ridgewood Industrial Park,

Uckfield, East Sussex,

TN22 5QE England

Tel: +44 (0) 1825 749494

www.naval-military-press.com

www.nmarchive.com

This diary has been reprinted in facsimile from the original. Any imperfections are inevitably reproduced and the quality may fall short of modern type and cartographic standards.

© **Crown Copyright**
Images reproduced by permission of The National Archives, London, England, 2015.

Contents

Document type	Place/Title	Date From	Date To
Heading	57th Division C.R.A. Feb 1917-Mar 1919 1915 Aug-1916 Jan 1917 Feb-1919 Mar		
Heading	WO95/2968-1		
Miscellaneous	General Statement. Period 1st August To 31st August 1915	04/09/1915	04/09/1915
Heading	War Diary Of Headquarters 2/1st West Lancashire Divisional Artillery T.F. From 1st September 1915. To 30th September 1915		
War Diary	Weeton	06/09/1915	18/09/1915
War Diary	Canterbury	19/09/1915	23/09/1915
Miscellaneous	War Diary Headquarters 2/1st West Lancashire Divisional Artillery T.F.		
War Diary		02/10/1915	28/10/1915
Heading	War Diary Of 57th (2/1st West Lancs) Divisional Artillery T.F. For Month Of November 1915		
War Diary		02/11/1915	30/11/1915
Heading	War Diary Of Headquarters 57th (2/1st West Lancs) Divisional Artillery. For December 1915		
War Diary		01/12/1915	30/12/1915
Heading	War Diary Royal Artillery Headquarters, 57th (West Lancs) Division, From 1st January 1916, To 31st January 1916		
War Diary	Canterbury	04/01/1916	31/01/1916
Heading	War Diary Of Headquarters Royal Artillery 57th (West Lancs) Division. For Month Of February 1916		
War Diary	Canterbury	08/02/1916	08/02/1916
War Diary	Ashford	18/02/1916	18/02/1916
War Diary	Faversham	19/02/1916	19/02/1916
War Diary	Canterbury	21/02/1916	21/02/1916
War Diary	Thanington	22/02/1916	22/02/1916
War Diary	Canterbury	24/02/1916	28/02/1916

57TH DIVISION

C. R. A.

~~FEB 1917 - MAR 1919~~

1915 AUG — 1916 JAN
+
1917 FEB — 1919 MAR

WD95/2968(1)

GENERAL STATEMENT.
Period 1st August to 31st August 1915.

Unit.   R.A. Headquarters.

Division. 57th (West Lancs.) Division.

Temporary War Station.   Canterbury.

Mobilization Centre.   Liverpool.

(a) Mobilization.   —

(b) Concentration at War Station.   —

(c) Organization for Defence.   Units are practically devoid of carbines.

(d) Training.   Continual courses take place in Telephony, Farriery, Signalling Wheelers Work, and Saddlery, Rough Riding, Cable Laying and the use of the Telephone Cart.
Operations took place on Aug. 23, 24, 25 and 26th with the 2nd Canadian Division.

(e) Discipline. Good.

(f) Administration.
1. Medical Services.   Good.
2. Veterinary.   Good.
3. Supply Services.   Satisfactory. Oats supplied are still of a poor quality.
4. Transport Services.   —
5. Ordnance Services.   Satisfactory. Watercarts are still urgently needed. A quantity of new harness has been received but still more is required and a great quantity of Govt. Pattern harness in possesion is fast becoming unserviceable. Telephone equipment is also urgently needed.
6. Billeting & Hutting.   Satisfactory.
7. Channel of correspondence in routine matter.   —
8. Range Construction.   —
9. Supply of Remounts.   Better but about 230 horses are still required to complete the Div. Arty.

(g) Reorganization of T.F. into Home and Imperial Service.   Complete.

(h) Preparation of Units for Imperial Service.   Complete except as regards equipment.

Brig.-Gen
(West Lancashire)

CRA 57 DIV

CONFIDENTIAL.

WAR DIARY

- of -

HEADQUARTERS

2/1ST WEST LANCASHIRE DIVISIONAL ARTILLERY, T. F.

From :- 1st September 1915.

To :- 30th September 1915.

Wincheap House,
Canterbury.
6th Oct. 1915.

[signature] COLONEL, R.A.,
COMMANDING 2/1st WEST LANCASHIRE DIVISIONAL ARTILLERY, T.F.

Army Form C. 2118.

WAR DIARY
INTELLIGENCE SUMMARY
(Erase heading not required.) SEPTEMBER, 1915.

Instructions regarding War Diaries and Intelligence Summaries are contained in F. S. Regs., Part II. and the Staff Manual respectively. Title pages will be prepared in manuscript.

Hour, Date, Place	Summary of Events and Information	Remarks and references to Appendices
Weeton, 6th September, 1915.	Instructions received to send Advance Parties of three Officers and 100 men from 2/1st Brigade, 2/2nd Brigade, 2/3rd Brigade, to Ash, Kennington and Faversham respectively.	
Weeton, 7th September, 1915.	Instructions received to send Advance Party of 2/8th Battery to Luton, and 2/9th Battery to Dorking.	
Weeton, 7th September, 1915	Advance Parties left Weeton accordingly.	
Weeton, 13th September, 1915	Capt. Townsend, Staff Captain, proceeded to Canterbury to administer 2nd Line Units.	
Weeton, 16th September, 1915. 11-15 p.m.	2/1st West Lancs. F. A. Brigade proceeded to Ash and Eastry.	
Weeton, 17th September, 1915. 11-15 p.m.	2/2nd West Lancs. F. A. Brigade proceeded to Kennington, near Ashford.	
Weeton, 18th September, 1915. 11-15 p.m.	Headquarters, 2/1st West Lancs. Divisional Artillery proceeded to Canterbury; 2/3rd West Lancs. F. A. Brigade proceeded to Faversham.	
Canterbury, 19th Sept.1915 11-15 a.m.	Headquarters, 2/1st West Lancs. Divisional Artillery arrived Canterbury.	
Canterbury, 23rd Sept. 1915.	Headquarters, 2/1st West Lancs. Divisional Artillery took over offices and documents at Wincheap House, Canterbury, from Headquarters, 57th (West Lancs.) Divisional Artillery.	

G.Wm.Taylor
Col. R.A.
Comdg 2/1st West Lancs Div: A.?

CONFIDENTIAL WAR DIARY.

Headquarters,

2/1st West Lancashire Divisional Artillery, T.F.

*****

Wincheap House,
CANTERBURY,
6th November, 1915.

[signature] Colonel, R.A.,
Commanding 2/1st West Lancashire
Divisional Artillery, T.F.

Army Form C. 2118.

WAR DIARY
~~INTELLIGENCE SUMMARY~~
(Erase heading not required.)

Instructions regarding War Diaries and Intelligence Summaries are contained in F. S. Regs, Part II. and the Staff Manual respectively. Title pages will be prepared in manuscript.

Hour, Date, Place	Summary of Events and Information	Remarks and references to Appendices
2nd October, 1915.	C.R.A. visited 2/2nd West Lancs. F. A. Brigade at Kennington. Inspected Horses, A.D.V.S. being present. Inspected rear gun emplacements for anti-aircraft purposes. Proceeded thence to Faversham.	
3rd do.	Instructions received from Headquarters that maximum quadrant elevation for 15 pdrs. was 23° when used for anti-aircraft purposes.	
5th do.	C.R.A. went to London to see General Bethune on various matters concerning the 2nd Line Artillery.	
7th do.	C.R.A. and Capt. Townsend visited Margate and selected various gun positions for 90 mm. guns in conjunction with Brig.Gen. H.Martin and R.E.Officer.	
9th do.	Capt. Townsend proceeded to Great Chart and Charing to inspect billets for horses and men of 2/2nd West Lancs. F. A. Brigade.	
11th do.	Capt. Townsend proceeded to Ashford to arrange classes of instruction for Wheelwrights with Mr. Maunsell, Manager, S.E. & C.Rly. Inspected billets and stabling in neighbourhood of Kennington.	
12th do.	C.R.A. saw Gen. Forster and arranged for visit to Coast to select positions with Capt. Tavenner (O.C., 9th Prov. Battery).	
13th do.	C.R.A. & Capt. Townsend visited Coast line and selected positions for 90 mm. Guns: final approval to be given by Gen. Martin. Capt. Tavenner, O.C., 9th Prov. Battery, present. Zeppelin raid began 9-30 p.m. 2/1st, 2/2nd and 2/3rd West Lancs. F. A. Brigades turned out ready to fire: drivers stood to.	
14th do.	Capt. Townsend proceeded to London to arrange Course of Instruction for Wheelers at S.E. & C. Rly. Bricklayers Arms Station. Also Course of Instruction at School of Cookery, London. Arrangements made at Union Jack Club and Duke of Connaught's Club respectively for accommodation.	

(1).

Army Form C. 2118.

WAR DIARY

INTELLIGENCE SUMMARY

(Erase heading not required.)

Instructions regarding War Diaries and Intelligence Summaries are contained in F. S. Regs., Part II. and the Staff Manual respectively. Title pages will be prepared in manuscript.

Hour, Date, Place	Summary of Events and Information	Remarks and references to Appendices
19th October, 1915.	Received letter from 2nd Army re Gun positions (2 p.m.).	
20th do.	C.R.A. saw General Staff and arranged that Capt. Tavenner would reconnoitre and select new positions for 90 mm. Guns which would afterwards be inspected by C.R.A.	
21st do.	C.R.A. visited Faversham, Ash and Eastry with Col. Boddam of the General Staff to inspect arrangements made for using 15 pdrs. as anti-aircraft Guns. 182 horses arrived from Avonmouth.	
22nd do.	Capt. Townsend visited Eastry, Ash with Col. Panton re messing arrangements. R.A. Units took over 182 horses from Wincheap. These had come from Avonmouth and were distributed as follows:- 2/1st Bde. 70; 2/2nd Bde. 40; 2/3rd Bde. 60; 2/4th Bde. 12; 100 mules met by 2/4th Bde. C.R.A. attended General Court Martial.	
23rd do.	C.R.A. attended General Court Martial. O.C., 2/3rd Bde. reported that about 40 out of 60 horses received have got ringworm. This matter reported to A.D.V.S. who will inspect on 25th October.	
25th do.	A.D.V.S. inspected 60 horses of 2/3rd Bde. 35 of these have ringworm and are to be treated at Faversham.	
27th do.	Zeppelin raid reported. Brigades turned out but nothing happened. Orderly Officer, 2/3rd Bde. reported that he heard the sound of engines.	
28th do.	C.R.A. and Capt. Townsend visited Kennington, Great Chart, Charing and Faversham to inspect billeting accommodation of 2nd and 3rd Brigades.	

Confidential

War Diary

of

57th (2/1st West Lancs) Divisional
Artillery. T.F.

for month of

November, 1915.

Moorheab Avenue,
Canterbury.
6/12/15.

W.M. Taylor. Capt. R.A.
Comdg 57th (2/1st West Lancs)
Divisional Artillery.

Army Form C. 2118.

WAR DIARY
or
INTELLIGENCE SUMMARY
(Erase heading not required.)

Instructions regarding War Diaries and Intelligence Summaries are contained in F. S. Regs., Part II. and the Staff Manual respectively. Title pages will be prepared in manuscript.

Hour, Date, Place	Summary of Events and Information	Remarks and references to Appendices
November 2nd 1915	Lieut. R.B. Goldie 2/1st Lancs Battery R.F.A. appointed Staff Captain 57th (2/1st West Lancashire) Divisional Artillery as from September 17th.	
November 4th 1915	6. R.A. and Brigade Major proceeded to Chiltolehe at met G.O.C. 2nd Army; G.O.C. 57th Division and G.O.C. 9th Provisional Brigade: inspected trades of suggested gun position.	
November 6th 1915.	G.O.C., C.R.A., B.M. Journed, Brigade Major Journed to Sherbourne. Attended Rehearse Course of Instruction at School of Gunnery Sherburgen.	
November 6th 1915. 11.35 p.m.	Message received by telephone from Headquarters 57th Division that the wireless of both aircraft had been heard at Shottery north of Harwich. Message related to Zepp Brigades.	
November 7th 1915. 9.45 a.m.	Code message warning against Zeppelin raid in near future. Later message related Zeppelins at Rye and Clenbery Norfolk.	

1247 W 3299 200,000 (E) 8/13 J.B.C. & A. Form/C. 2118/11.

WAR DIARY
or
INTELLIGENCE SUMMARY

(Erase heading not required.)

Army Form C. 2118.

Instructions regarding War Diaries and Intelligence Summaries are contained in F. S. Regs., Part II. and the Staff Manual respectively. Title pages will be prepared in manuscript.

Hour, Date, Place	Summary of Events and Information	Remarks and references to Appendices
Nov 8th 1915.	Lieut. Col. Parker inspected 1/1st Lancs Battery R.F.A.	
Nov 9th 1915.	Lieut Col. Parker continued his inspection of the said unit	
Nov 10th 1915.	C.R.A. visited Faversham and inspected 2/4th Lancs Battery R.F.A.	
Nov 11th 1915.	Col. Pratt Assistant Inspector of Remounts visited Hannington and inspected horses and personnel of 2/4th West Lancs F.A. Hers. Brigade and 1/1st Lancs Battery R.F.A. A lecture to both units was delivered.	
Nov 12th 1915.	Col. Pratt Assistant Inspector of Remounts inspected horses and personnel of 2/2nd West Lancs F.A. Brigade and 2/3rd West Lancs F.A. Brigade at Faversham. Lecture was delivered to all units.	
Nov 15th 1915.	D.A.Q.M.G. 59th Division inspected horses and vehicles of 2/3rd Brigade at Faversham.	

Army Form C. 2118.

WAR DIARY
or
INTELLIGENCE SUMMARY
(Erase heading not required.)

Instructions regarding War Diaries and Intelligence Summaries are contained in F. S. Regs., Part II. and the Staff Manual respectively. Title pages will be prepared in manuscript.

Hour, Date, Place	Summary of Events and Information	Remarks and references to Appendices
November 16th 1915	D.A.G.M.S. 57th Division inspected horses and vehicles of 2/2 Brigade at Winchester.	
November 15th 1915	Horse lines moved Grangeford to Provisional Battalion at Mount at Maryh.	
November 18th 1915	G.O.C. 2nd Army inspected 2/3rd Brigade at Faversham.	
November 20th 1915	Lieut. E. Hall 2/2nd Brigade; Lieut. A. M. Jacob 2/3rd Brigade; Lt. Col. D.G. Cann 2/1st Brigade. See Lieut. P.F. Moffatt 2/4th Brigade proceeded to Southampton for attachment to British Expeditionary Force for Instruction days.	
Nov 22nd 1915	See Lieut. S.E. Groode 2/2nd Brigade and 30 N.C.O's and men proceeded London to attend course of instruction in Cold Shoeing at Borough Polytechnic Institute S.E. 10. N.C.O's and men commenced course of instruction at Tonbridge in Saddlery. 28. N.C.O's and men commenced Course of Instruction in Schottmere at Bridge.	

Army Form C. 2118.

WAR DIARY
or
INTELLIGENCE SUMMARY
(Erase heading not required.)

Instructions regarding War Diaries and Intelligence Summaries are contained in F. S. Regs., Part II. and the Staff Manual respectively. Title pages will be prepared in manuscript.

Hour, Date, Place	Summary of Events and Information	Remarks and references to Appendices
November 22nd 1915.	G.R.A. forwarded to Estaly ad inspected 2/2 About Lancashire Batty. O.I.C. ad 2/1st Lancs Ammunition Column.	
November 23rd 1915	G.R.A. forwarded to Tunbridge Wells to see G.O.C. 2nd Army.	
November 27th 1915	Major General Brunker Inspector R.H. and R.F.G. inspected 2/4th Brigade Hannington	
November 29th 1915	Major General Brunker Inspector R.H. and R.F.G. inspected 2/2nd Brigade Vinninghs	
November 30th 1915.	Major General Brunker inspected 2/3rd Brigade at Faversham	

G. Mifflin Taylor Col. R.A.

Confidential
War Diary
of
Headquarters
57th (2/1st West Lancs) Divisional Artillery.
for
December 1915.

Wincheap House,
Canterbury.
5th January 1916.

E.W.M. Taylor Lt. Col. R.A.

WAR DIARY
or
INTELLIGENCE SUMMARY

(Erase heading not required.)

Army Form C. 2118.

Hour, Date, Place	Summary of Events and Information	Remarks and references to Appendices
Dec. 1st. 1915.	Major-General Brooker inspected 2/1st Brigade at Ash + Eastry. Col. Lomas A.S.C. inspected horses + equipment of the 2/2nd Brigade at Kennington. G.O.C. 2nd Army inspected 2/1st Howitzer Brigade at Thanington.	
Dec. 3rd. --	C.R.A. inspected Lancs. Battery (2/1st Bde.). 3 18 pdr. guns received by 2/1st Battery. 3 18 pdr. guns received by 2/1st Battery. 4 18 pdr. guns received by 2/9th Battery. 3 18 pdr. guns received by 2/2nd Battery. 4 18 pdr. guns received by 2/10th Battery. 3 18 pdr. guns received by 2/3rd Battery.	
Dec. 6th --	C.R.A. inspected 13th Lancs. Battery, saw men's messing, stables + c/o at office.	

Army Form C. 2118.

WAR DIARY
or
INTELLIGENCE SUMMARY

(Erase heading not required.)

Instructions regarding War Diaries and Intelligence Summaries are contained in F. S. Regs., Part II. and the Staff Manual respectively. Title pages will be prepared in manuscript.

Hour, Date, Place	Summary of Events and Information	Remarks and references to Appendices
Dec. 7th 1915.	Capt. Nixon inspected Signallers at Faversham + Kennington also Horses of 2/1st Bde R.F.A. 2/4th Bde. + 2/1st Henry Battery Concentrated at Thanington.	
Dec. 8th — —	4 18 pdr. guns received by 2/1 Lancs. Battery.	
Dec. 9th — —	12 18 pdr. guns received by 2/3rd Bde. at Faversham.	
Dec. 13th — —	Inspector of Ordnance Machinery inspected guns + equipment of 2/3rd West Lancs. F.A. Bde.	
Dec. 14th — —	Inspector of Ordnance Machinery inspected guns + equipment of Ash & Battery of 2/1st F.A. Bde.	
Dec. 15th — —	Inspector of Ordnance Machinery inspected guns + equipment at Kennington of 2/2 Bde R.F.A.	
Dec. 16th — —	Inspector of Ordnance Machinery inspected guns + equipment of 2/4th Brigade & 1/1st Lancs. Battery, R.G.A. at Thanington.	

WAR DIARY
or
INTELLIGENCE SUMMARY

(Erase heading not required.)

Army Form C. 2118.

Hour, Date, Place	Summary of Events and Information	Remarks and references to Appendices
Dec. 16th 1915	C.R.A. inspected 2/4th Bde at Thenington.	
Dec. 17th ""	C.R.A. inspected 2/3rd Battery at Bustory.	
Dec. 18th ""	Four guns of 2/1st Bde (15pdrs) proceeded to Lydd to be used for practice by (two Centrice) 67th Sie. Artillery.	
Dec. 20th ""	Brigade Major visited C.O.O. Seven barrage for examination of the 15pdr. guns at Lydd. Major Burrell Inspector Remounts visited Thenington & inspected horses of 2/4th West Lancs F.A. (Honor) Bde. 1/1st Lancs Battery R.G.A. 2/1st Lancs Battery R.G.A.	
Dec. 21st ""	Brigade Major proceeded to Lydd to make arrangements as to Gunnery Practice by 57th West Lancs. Sie. Artillery.	
Dec. 22nd ""	Instructions received 9/Artillery/8881.M. that 1/1st Lancs Heavy Battery & Ammunition Column are to proceed to Woolwich to be mobilised for service in France. Move to Woolwich to be carried out not later than 29th inst-	

Army Form C. 2118.

WAR DIARY
or
INTELLIGENCE SUMMARY

(Erase heading not required.)

Instructions regarding War Diaries and Intelligence Summaries are contained in F. S. Regs., Part II. and the Staff Manual respectively. Title pages will be prepared in manuscript.

Hour, Date, Place	Summary of Events and Information	Remarks and references to Appendices
3.25. a.m. Dec. 25th/9/15.	Message received by Telephone warning that a daylight raid by hostile Aircraft might possibly be expected. Later message stated that Naval & Military flights had been arranged & that if fired upon two Verey's lights would be dropped. Messages passed to all Brigades.	
Dec. 28th --	1/1st Lancs Battery. R.G.A. proceeded from Harwich to Woolwich.	
Dec. 30th --	Message received from H.Q. 57th Div. reporting message from Secretary that Major J. D. G. McMillan R.A. is appointed Brigade Major 57th (2nd West Lancs.) Div. Artillery.	

G. Griffin. Maj. RA CO 71A

Confidential.

War Diary
of
Royal Artillery Headquarters,
57th (West Lancs:) Division.

From 1st January 1916, to 31st January 1916.

Army Form C. 2118.

Headquarters, Royal Artillery,
67th (2nd Lancs.) Division.

WAR DIARY
or
INTELLIGENCE SUMMARY
(Erase heading not required.)

Instructions regarding War Diaries and Intelligence Summaries are contained in F. S. Regs., Part II. and the Staff Manual respectively. Title pages will be prepared in manuscript.

Hour, Date, Place	Summary of Events and Information	Remarks and references to Appendices
CANTERBURY, 4.1.16	Major J. STC. MACMILLAN, R.F.A. Res. of Off., arrived and assumed duty as Brigade Major vice Major C.V.M. TOWNSEND.	Sgr.
5.1.16	Routine.	Sgr.
6.1.16	2/1st Brigade moved from ASH and EASTRY to THANINGTON HUTMENTS. 2/4th (How.) Brigade moved from THANINGTON HUTMENTS to WINGHAM - its 13th Ammunition Column to PRESTON. Brig-General F.B. ELMSLIE, C.B., arrived to assume command vice Colonel G.F. KYFFIN-TAYLOR, T.F.	Sgr.
7.1.16 and 8.1.16	2/2nd Brigade carried out gun practice with 15 Pr. B.L.C. equipment at LYDD. Billeted at RYE.	Sgr.
10.1.16 and 11.1.16	2/3rd Brigade carried out gun practice with 15 Pr. B.L.C. equipment at LYDD. Billeted at RYE.	Sgr.
12.1.16	C.R.A. and Brigade Major visited 2/4th (Howitzer) Brigade at WINGHAM.	Sgr.
13.1.16	C.R.A. and Brigade Major visited 2/2nd Brigade and inspected billets etc. at KENNINGTON, GREAT CHART, CHARING, and BOUGHTON LEES.	Sgr.

1247 W 3299 200,000 (E) 8/14 J.B.C. & A.   Forms/C. 2118/11.

Army Form C. 2118.

WAR DIARY
or
INTELLIGENCE SUMMARY

(Erase heading not required.)

Instructions regarding War Diaries and Intelligence Summaries are contained in F.S. Regs, Part II. and the Staff Manual respectively. Title pages will be prepared in manuscript.

Hour, Date, Place	Summary of Events and Information	Remarks and references to Appendices
14.1.16	C.R.A. visited 2/3rd Brigade at FAVERSHAM; saw rides, gun drill, billets and stables; also inspected anti-aircraft arrangements. Brigade Major visited 2/4th (Howitzer) Brigade at WINGHAM, saw Alarm Parade, also inspected billets of Ammunition Column at PRESTON.	JHy.
15.1.16	Lieut-Col. R.C. Drury reported for duty & assumed command of 2/3rd Brigade vice Lieut-Col. G.W. GOSSAGE.	Authority W.O. letter No 39140/3, dt. 12.1.16. JHy.
17.1.16	C.R.A. visited 2/1st Brigade at THANINGTON. 3 p.m. All O.s.C. Brigades at Headquarters for Conference with C.R.A.	JHy.
18.1.16	C.R.A. visited 2/1st Brigade at THANINGTON. Brigade Major proceeded to CHILHAM to superintend transfer of 688 rounds 18 Pr Q.F. ammunition from 2/1st Bde Ammunition Column to 2/2nd do: Inchecheck guns on limbers noticed, also march discipline and turn-out.	JHy.
19.1.16	C.R.A. visited 2/1st Brigade at THANINGTON.	JHy.

Army Form C. 2118.

WAR DIARY
or
INTELLIGENCE SUMMARY
(Erase heading not required.)

Instructions regarding War Diaries and Intelligence Summaries are contained in F. S. Regs., Part II. and the Staff Manual respectively. Title pages will be prepared in manuscript.

Hour, Date, Place	Summary of Events and Information	Remarks and references to Appendices
20.1.16	C.R.A. visited 2/3rd Brigade at FAVERSHAM. Brigade Major visited 2/1st Brigade at THANINGTON and gave instruction in Manoeuvre.	
21.1.16	Orders received to bring Establishment up to "War Establishments Part VIII" (as amended by "War Establh. of Artillery Units" dated 15.12.15) plus 10 per cent of other Ranks. Major J.C. STITT, who had proceeded to LIVERPOOL on 19.1.16, on transfer from Command of 2/1st Lancs. Battery, R.G.A., to that of 57th Divisional Ammunition Column established Headquarters of latter at THE DRILL SHED, RATHBONE ROAD, OLD SWAN, LIVERPOOL, and proceeded to arrange for raising of the Divisional Ammunition Column.	
23.1.16	Messages received of Enemy air raid on DOVER. Anti-aircraft guns of 2/2nd Brigade, KENNINGTON, and 2/3rd Brigade, FAVERSHAM, manned.	

1247 W 3299 200,000 (E) 8/14 J.B.C. & A. Forms/C.2118/11.

Army Form C. 2118.

WAR DIARY
or
INTELLIGENCE SUMMARY

(Erase heading not required.)

Instructions regarding War Diaries and Intelligence Summaries are contained in F. S. Regs., Part II. and the Staff Manual respectively. Title pages will be prepared in manuscript.

Hour, Date, Place	Summary of Events and Information	Remarks and references to Appendices
24.1.16 9.15 a.m.	C.R.A. visited 2/1st Brigade at THANINGTON. Later, left with Brigade Major for FAVERSHAM, where he was joined by O.C. and Adjutant of 2/3rd Brigade and proceeded to inspect artillery positions along coast line from GRAVENEY MARSHES to RECULVER. Flight Sub-Lieut. LACEY, R.N., landed in field adjoining THANINGTON camp, with balloon "SPARROW". Aircraft passage resumed. 2/1st, 2/2nd and 2/3rd Brigades informed, & detachments turned out.	O.K.
25.1.16	C.R.A. inspected 2/2nd (How.) Brigade and Ammn Column in GOODNESTONE PARK. Brigade Major gave instruction in manoeuvre to 2/3rd Brigade at THANINGTON.	
6.25 p.m.	2/1st Brigade reported having seen what appeared to be arc-light to S.W. between CHARTHAM and HARDRES WOOD. Divisional H.Q. at once informed by telephone.	O.K.

1247 W 3259 200,000 (E) 8/15 J.B.C. & A. Forms/C. 2118/11.

Army Form C. 2118.

WAR DIARY
or
INTELLIGENCE SUMMARY
(Erase heading not required.)

Instructions regarding War Diaries and Intelligence Summaries are contained in F. S. Regs, Part. II. and the Staff Manual respectively. Title pages will be prepared in manuscript.

Hour, Date, Place	Summary of Events and Information	Remarks and references to Appendices
26.1.16	C.R.A. visited 2/1st Brigade at THANINGTON.	
27.1.16	Inspection of 2/2nd Brigade by C.R.A. at CHALLOCK LEES, in F.S.M.O., at Ceremonial and Manoeuvre.	
28.1.16	Inspection of 2/1st Lowland (Heavy) Battery at OLD PARK. Puckeridge Messages (attached) received between 1.15 p.m. and 11.33 p.m. Anti-aircraft details. Parts of 2/1st, 2/2nd, and 2/3rd Brigades turned out. Dismissed at 11.45 p.m.	× App. I.
29.1.16	C.R.A. inspected books of 2/1st and 2/3rd Brigades.	
30.1.16	C.R.A. inspected books of 2/2nd Brigade. Brigade Major took 2/4th (Hows.) Brigade in mobile form in Ceremonial (mounted) at BARHAM DOWNS.	

G. B. Elworthy Comdt. R.A.
C.R.A. 57

Confidential

War Diary

~ of ~

Headquarters, Royal Artillery,
57th (West Lancs) Division.

~ for ~

month of February, 1916.

R.A. Headquarters,
Canterbury, March 1916.
2nd

G. B. Currie
Colonel, R.A.,
Commanding, Royal Artillery,
57th (West Lancs) Division.

Army Form C. 2118.

WAR DIARY
or
INTELLIGENCE SUMMARY
(Erase heading not required.)

Instructions regarding War Diaries and Intelligence Summaries are contained in F. S. Regs., Part II. and the Staff Manual respectively. Title pages will be prepared in manuscript.

Hour, Date, Place	Summary of Events and Information	Remarks and references to Appendices
CANTERBURY. 8.2.16	Lt Col A.W.B. GORDON RFA assumed command of 2/1st Brigade.	H.Q.R.
ASHFORD ~~FAVERSHAM~~ 18.2.16	Inspection by Inspector R.H. & R.F.A. of 2/2nd Brigade. General remarks – Quite satisfactory.	H.Q.R.
FAVERSHAM 19.2.16	Inspection by Inspector R.H. & R.F.A. of 2/3rd Brigade. Remarks. Gun Drill & Fuze Discipline 2/10th & 2/11th very poor.	H.Q.R.
CANTERBURY 21.2.16	Inspection by Inspector R.H. & R.F.A. of 2/4th Brigade & 2/1st Lancs Battery R.F.A. Special Remarks – Redus manoeuvre & gun drill show a want of supervision over training of Brigade by C.O.	H.Q.R.
THANINGTON. 22.2.16	Inspection by Inspector R.H. & R.F.A. of 2/1st Brigade. General Remarks:- Considerable improvement.	H.Q.R.
CANTERBURY. 24.2.16	Instructions received to hold 2 batteries in readiness to proceed by road or rail in case of a raid between WHITSTABLE & DEAL.	H.Q.R.

Army Form C. 2118.

WAR DIARY
or
INTELLIGENCE SUMMARY

(Erase heading not required.)

Instructions regarding War Diaries and Intelligence Summaries are contained in F. S. Regs., Part II. and the Staff Manual respectively. Title pages will be prepared in manuscript.

Hour, Date, Place	Summary of Events and Information	Remarks and references to Appendices
CANTERBURY. 26.2.16	Major J. St C. MACMILLAN proceeded to LONDON to take up duties of G.S.O. III Home Forces.	
	Lt Col G. MILNE, C.B., V.D. R.A. assumed command of the 2/1st Brigade.	H.F.R.
28.2.16	Captain H.F. REW assumed duties of Staff Captain vice Lt N.B. GOLDIE	H.F.R.

www.ingramcontent.com/pod-product-compliance
Lightning Source LLC
Chambersburg PA
CBHW081504160426
43193CB00014B/2590